HEARTLAND

for Mark, always

HEARTLAND
MICHELE LEGGOTT

AUCKLAND
UNIVERSITY
PRESS

I wish to thank the following people: David Eggleton for permission to quote from his poem 'Matariki from Takarunga'. The Auckland taxi driver whose voice supplies the third part of 'ngā kaitiaki / the guardians'. Clive Saleman and Libby Baker for their help in locating Edward and Elizabeth Evans' Taranaki land purchases on Maude Road in the Hua and Waiwhakaiho Block. Bram Evans for his help in ascertaining what happened to one of two brothers who survived the conflict of 1914–18, only to die in England a year later in mysterious circumstances. The brothers were our grandfathers, Arthur Owen Evans, FRCS (Edinburgh), and Edward Douglas (Argoyd) Evans.

Quotation from Robin Hyde's 1937 writings about Northland appear in 'spirits bay'. Edward Percy Cox's Gallipoli diary and the regimental histories of the New Zealand Mounted Rifles supplement family records used in the composition of 'some day'.

Some of these poems have appeared in *All Together Now: A Digital Bridge for Auckland and Sydney, Antipodes: A Global Journal of Australian/New Zealand Literature, Best New Zealand Poems, Brief, Cordite Poetry Review, foam:e, Frankfurt Bookfair 2012: An Aotearoa Affair, JAAM, Landfall, Mascara Literary Review, Metro, A Million Poems for Matariki*, the New Zealand Poet Laureate website, *Otoliths, Seven Stars, Snorkel, Southerly*, the *Tuesday Poem* website, *Turbine* and *The Winding Stair*. Five were published in 2010 as *northland*, a chapbook from Pania Press, and 'lomu' was a Phantom Billstickers poem poster in 2013.

First published 2014

Auckland University Press
University of Auckland
Private Bag 92019
Auckland 1142
New Zealand
www.press.auckland.ac.nz

© Michele Leggott, 2014

ISBN 978 1 86940 808 4

National Library of New Zealand Cataloguing-in-Publication Data
Leggott, Michele J.
Heartland / Michele Leggott.
ISBN 978-1-86940-808-4
I. Title.
NZ821.2—dc 23

Publication is assisted by creative nz
ARTS COUNCIL OF NEW ZEALAND TOI AOTEAROA

This book is copyright. Apart from fair dealing for the purpose of private study, research, criticism or review, as permitted under the Copyright Act, no part may be reproduced by any process without prior permission of the publisher.
The moral rights of the author have been asserted.

Cover design: Keely O'Shannessy
Cover photograph: the *Gairloch* wreck. Dean Mullin, www.deanmullinphotography.com
Page 114 photograph: the *Gairloch*, built 1884 for the Northern Steamship Company Ltd.
Allan Kirk Collection, Voyager New Zealand Maritime Museum

Printed by 1010 Printing International Ltd

Contents

a little ahead, my shadow   1
  as the car flies   2
  forget about paper   3
  one hundred days   4
  little eyes   5
  te tōrea / the oystercatcher   7
  another matariki song   9
  the answers   11
  te oru / the stingray   13
  tiger moth   15
  finding isabella   17
  thomas who was a soldier   19

unwinding the bird   21
  spirits bay   22
  listening   24
  fat buds   26
  degli angeli   28
  never dreaming   29
  circadia   31
  heartland   33
  ngā kaitiaki / the guardians   34
  land sea and sky   36
  the longest night   38

many hands   41

the mezzaluna rocking	59
the digger and the faun	60
after the war	61
harbour lights	63
lomu	64
olive	65
honey meadow	67
dear sister anne	68
jackson's road	70
frederick walter	72
experiments (our life together)	74
talking to the sky	76
a brief history of time	78
some day	81
wind and weather	99
matapouri	111
Note	113

A LITTLE AHEAD, MY SHADOW

as the car flies

it's no distance to the orchard
where Mrs D asks her son   how many left
and his voice from the darkness of the shed
maybe a couple of weeks   these were on the tree
yesterday   we take two bags and head back
to the city   leaving you to have a lie down
and rethread the silence that preceded
our visit   my friend you are a voice
against a dark red wall and we have covered
the important and unimportant things
that brought us to your door   last tomatoes
next book   a sunny room where white gloves
bring huge prints from their envelopes
we take letters to post and you give directions
to Dragicevichs'   *sweet, crisp*
there are no other words   the trip you will make
into the northern summer   and the return
you stand in sunlight beside the small car
no longer invisible   and when we say goodbye
I am holding an armful of peonies

forget about paper

these are my two in the city
one calls across an intersection
and away we go   wheeling his bike
to meet the other   who patrols
outside Invito in its perpetual war
with Mecca   the stick is picking up drifts
of leaves   papery fallen petals
and the sun is still warm on my back
one sits   one stands   eyes flicking
over the pavement as they compare
the lunch rush and arrange a drink
after work   one rides off into the traffic
I walk on and collect a lens   ever more
incongruous at the optometrists but they
play along   soon I'm crossing
another intersection and this time
a violin is talking to a crowd of people
who throw notes and coins
into an open case   hot jazz
afternoon sun and the singer
blind but not for one moment
in doubt   the way you look tonight
stealing up the sides of glass towers
or cutting the corner on a red light
they are my two   I don't have
to worry and we can forget
about paper   except as tissue
memory drifting from trees
in the thumpety heart of the city

one hundred days

thick drifts of leaves   soft
percussion of counting apples
in a basket   the Oratia Kid tied on
his hankie and went to town   look
he said   two bellybuttons   this is where
they put the camera in   applause
from the table and indeed the street
the Yorkshireman with yoghurt on a spoon
laughing fit to bust   the poet
who's had visitors from Mexico City
perched in his spare room   what the hell
leaves fall thick and fast   HOPE
says the t-shirt   the floors of memory
proliferate and the café hums
something catchy under
its red bandana   almost one hundred
days and we are coming through
the valley with our apples
in golden drifts   along the road
sun pours into Alleluya's lantern
one hundred days and every one
a poem for the Kid and his buttons
pressed up against the dark

little eyes

two coffees to go
to Maungauika   above us
the golden bee of the sun
between us the basket   its blanket
and your sleeping head   little dog
you loved this hill   its spiral road
and the grass ghosts singing
in our ears   now you are still
and everything familiar is still
aching   except that black dot
on the horizon   no longer old
and free at last of the slow
obscenity lymphoma
delivered into your trusting body
last night you fell at my feet
and I knew it was over   little dog
you slept one last time
and then we woke you   one last time
there is much to say up here
on the hill   watching you
get further and further away
a frangipani blossom
and a white ginger flower
we will put you into the ground
between the avocado and the tītoki
where you stuck your nose
every morning
into the leaves and snorted for joy
white ginger and frangipani
go with you   last things   a shot

of cat food and your head
in my hands   love uncloses your eyes
and you see clearly again   little dog
chasing the golden bee of the sun
yes   run over that valley
and chase the birds into the sky

te tōrea / the oystercatcher

trebling stage left
and how would you ever
pick them out on the rocks
until they move and orange sticks
poke and shrill at the kids   who want
food and probably flying lessons
same old same   old tōrea   not in
Native Animals of New Zealand
but certainly one of the cards torn
from the jelly crystal packets each week
always three and often duplicates
what were we learning and why is it stuck
in the active grid this morning
looking at Motukorea   their island   and Motuihe
where a goose jumped out of a boat
on new year's day and danced
for lettuce from a bucket   oh he's
too small to leave on the farm   they said
and rowed back out to the yacht
bobbing off Von Luckner's bay

dogs rode in the bows of kayaks
landing we supposed on other parts of
the island famous for its permeable approach
to security   Pearl chasing down the Moa
out there in the sparkling waters of the gulf
and they got all the way to the Kermadecs
with their charts sextant and radio
and their pantomime imperial flag   another story
outside the cordon of plastic ribbons

on the landward beach and a sign
DO NOT DISTURB THIS BIRD   gazing
absently out to sea just above
the highwater mark   a jelly card swap
an indigene without sound   and this book
trebling calling catching itself
on the black terraces above the tide

another matariki song

because of the lemony light
falling falling falling
because one step is a theatre
any time any place
dazzling in its troubadour take
on real life (that life)
because you are far away
and far and away the best
impression we have
a legend tangoing in the streets
of Buenos Aires   happy bonus airs
because because
we are taking the lemons in their tubs
inside now   a theatre
walking all the way to the end
of the earth the beginning
of the new year   oh because
our terracotta feet are warm
and our palombaro wings outspread
we will go to the dark city
on the other side of the earth
we will walk the streets and buy shoes
and hats   we will stay out there
and watch for our sisters
making their way to the station
because because
everywhere is a theatre and limonaia
is where our feet take us
walking walking walking
over the bridges and the dark

river how shall we say it
going to meet the sea   going
to meet the river of light
streaming over our heads

the answers

it looks impossible   but really
it happened   is happening   the tabletop
bright red and the little chairs
each with a decal on its creamy enamel
the continuous tea party
that seems to be taking place whenever
we look   whenever we ask
what was that   where are those baths
that merry go round she rides
with one of us   the plank and sawhorse
seesaw in the driveway   the baby
stomping along in the sunhat
with her mother and the mountain behind
is that her on the path with presents
and why are his fingers bandaged

it is the moving that matters
the two of us and her walking to camera
at Pukeiti   the waterwheel beating
along the cool ravine   or the Rinso box
and one of us running and jumping
under the clothesline   rocking the pram
one taking out the other with the business end
of a hobby horse   silent howling
swimming and getting stagily into the car
the circus the fire engine a donkey ride
at Ngamotu   Fishers' bach Dees' bach
Onaero Urenui Mokau   ordinary things
and behind them the extraordinary grief
of watching the toddler on the lawn
fall into her father's arms

tonight on the cold Wellington streets
I see them walk by   coats no longer over
their arms but the ring from Stewart Dawson's
glinting on her hand there   and on mine
and on mine here   extraordinary grief
and the answers we make
from distance which is no distance at all

te oru / the stingray

hot blue stars at the edge of the world
some like horses   some like music
and one has a saxophone
we've got chalk words and lots of food
we've got the saxophone
blowing us out to the edge of the world
where the poems are

orcas arrive in the harbour
hunting stingray   the researchers
who named them have tracked the pod
from the Kaipara and say it is unique
in taking on the rays   maybe   maybe not
the whales frolic all morning
and when an escaping stingray
soars on camera   *ray skips lunch*
with orca   an old story flaps into view
stingray in the boat   crew jumping about
trying to gaff it   the whacking tail   pain
my father's bandaged fingers
held up to the whirring camera   his salute
to the fish   to us   and to her

hot blue stars at the edge of the world
cool blue bird under the wharf
a new sun climbs into the sky

on this side of the harbour
the tug Wainui and her barge Moehau
are bringing in sand from Pākiri

for the beach at Torpedo Bay
a stingray cruises about the shins
of the kaumātua blessing the sand
the foreshore and the seabed
are not quiet places   who can say
what belongs to this green mountain
rearing out of the morning mist

hot blue stars   flash of wings
under the wharf   kingfisher   bird of omen
tell us how the sun lights the new moon
how kites with sting tails float over Ōrākei
how an old story encircles the gleaming bay

tiger moth

poetry is a crayfish   or two
packed in wood shavings   flying
home in a chillibox with my name on it
dear family it's been a long time
let's go hunting the past   in order
to find the future   you ask me
what poetry is   and I tell you about
the whale and her calf tracking in the gulf
the coastguard has been alerted
because boaties might collide with them
the Rimutaka Hill Road is closed
the Rimutaka Hill Road is always closed
a work in progress or a bit character
like the dairy giant Fonterra
or the prime minister John Key
who was on the same flight last night
the survivor of the wreck is wearing
a French naval uniform   no lies
at the end of a long week   *La Glorieuse*
for entente cordiale   *La Glorieuse*

the old man bought a couple of Tiger Moths
back in the day   topdressed and flew
supplies into the farm   four minutes more
daylight since the shortest day   dear family
one cray is lost in action   the other
will not make it past dinner time tonight
this is poetry   you make it happen
wherever there are ears eyes
and mouths   wherever we sit down

to add flying hours to the work
in progress   wherever dear family   we are
and the news comes in thick and fast

finding isabella

my name is Isabella Burroughs
I am a mist clearing for a moment
in the marriage papers of my sons
who sailed away and did not return
one was born in County Tipperary
one in Doncaster when the regiment
came marching home
between them sleeps the little one
from our time at Bee Hive Yard

my name is Hannah Isabella
daughter of Thomas and Isabella
my sister and brothers sailed away
one by one   I didn't see them again
though letters came and we wrote back
I was born in Gloucester not long before
the regiment left for Ireland   another
sister with half my name is buried there
we have our mother's eyes

my name is Isabella   daughter
of William and Catherine   grand-daughter
of Thomas and Isabella over the sea   niece
of Hannah Isabella   a spinster all her days
I am first-born in the new country
never married   and I returned
to find the old people in their place
before the war separated us

my name is Isabella Rose   daughter
of Harry and Eda Rose   grand-daughter
of William and Catherine   niece Bella
to aunt Bella home from her travels
and perched on a hill in Kelburn
I am second-born and married
my Nelson cousin   we farmed at Aria
in the King Country   I have two daughters
Jean Catherine and Margaret Lorna

my name is Isobel Jean   daughter
of Harry and Jess   grand-daughter
of Harry and Eda   great grand-daughter
of William and Catherine
I am a twin   blue-eyed and fair
to my brother's dark eyes and black hair
I died young   my brothers and sister
look for me in nieces and grandchildren
my little daughter couldn't be saved

my name is Isabella   daughter
sister niece mother aunt   Isabella May
Katherine Isobel   Isabella   Catherine Isabella
look for me in the photographs
eyes widening   the edge of a smile

thomas who was a soldier

I told them I was eighteen
and attested for a bounty of three pounds
sterling   they filled out the forms
and told me I was five foot six
I put my signature to that and gave it
no more thought   Liverpool was next
then over the sea to the Irish depots

we came and went   and I went
up the ranks   corporal when I married
her   sergeant when my boys were born
colour sergeant when I saw Portsmouth
with my youngest in arms
after Canada   there were nine mouths
to feed and the Famine not far
behind us   I took my cut and got caught
they court martialled me in Dublin
84 days imprisonment with hard labour
reduced to the rank and pay of a private
for taking one pound nine and fourpence
and three farthings from company pay

I traded 21 years 149 days
for a medical discharge and got out
it was difficult returning to Belton
the boys wore most of it   wanting
early instruction by godly parents
they got right away and never came back
now there are grandchildren
a picture arrives of a young man

in a band uniform   fair hair blue eyes
fresh complexion   he could be twenty
five foot nine and a half   full grown
after a couple of years with the Rifles
no scars or disfigurements   character
and conduct perhaps three Badges
looking over his shoulder where
a girl with bright hair is disappearing
into the village church

an armful of lilies   she was
to me   or moonlight on the Suir

UNWINDING THE BIRD

spirits bay

the joker in the orange vest
is baiting up an electric kontiki
his mate is in charge of the line
has been up here three years or more
working on the roads   Saturday off
and they want to try this side   the kontiki
is good though sometimes the breakers
hammer it   twenty five minutes
in the battery   enough to get a fair way out
fish for tea plan A or plan B   their mate
is surfcasting from rocks below the point
their ute has an orange light on top
the kontiki a little red flag   up on the ridge
a black horse watches us
then walks off into the mānuka

she went back to Te Paki   turned south
for the run down the beach   a comedy
with driftwood and tarpaulin under the wheels
tide coming in and they got the car out
marching chocolate and toheroa leaving behind
the swish of vague stars above ti-tree
scratched out lines on Exquisite Bond   trying
to see the flying-off place   the pathway
of spirits a rope and basket affair
pretty near worn through twenty years
back   trying to see past melancholy
love is your overwhelming theme   yes
but why leave it to the horse and the stars
or the line of white plumes shaking
out there where the currents meet

the gateway has been shifted
the buildings erased   only the lighthouse
remains near the end of the spirit pathway
where the prophet heard the snuffling   peropero
of the dead as they passed and saw
a great house above the cliffs   crash barriers
write on the cambered bends
of the new road   sealed now from the top
working back to the junction and perhaps
ten kilometres to go   the three capes
wrangle as they have always done
and down the cliff comes that old kahika
still holding fast to the rock and refusing
ever to flower   a destiny and a song

listening

pīhoihoi the spiralling song   a pipit
and who will give the skylark a name
to fling against the cliffs   I cannot see
but my ears are open   have been opened
to the song and its destinations
spiralling backwards into the abyss
from which we will emerge   shining shocking
ready to start on the long walk south
alpha and omega I am with you
but I have changed hands   ostriches
an olive farm big windbreaks small chalets
unwinding the bird in my throat

in the city of words the wild man
wakes and knows he must leave
the warm bed the arms that detain him
where he has always wanted to be
this is not romance but death   the city of words
plunged into darkness   swans clattering
into the sky above the lake   which gleams
and turns back to the beloved head
at rest in the room before dawn   the wild man
ungovernable and meek as milk
all in the opening of one eye   has left
us now   he is near the on ramp and won't stop
even for the lament his brother makes
from wood glue a guitar and a kick drum
even for the voice that has held him
so long where he wanted to be
and now reaches into the sky   wordless

black wings crying   love pain hunger
I have changed hands alpha and omega
unwinding the bird in my throat

kōtare out the car window   here
wraith blossom and scrub cattle   there
dustclouds on the way to the fish farm
gone bust by the shallow harbour
one kōtare two kōtare three kōtare four
songlines for idiot ears   everywhere
velocity in the November sun
dog snuffling its way around a bend
gamboge yellow   not sure how much
to take literally   and what can be left
for the others   orange cones
fill my eyes on the road south   alpha
and omega changing hands   unwinding
the bird in my throat

fat buds

Oihi and the little rose
that drew us back to the museum
the historian's papers and Richard Taylor
boating along to Te Puna   the journal
on its cushion under creamy light   the abode
of civilised man in ruins again   already
strange carvings sunk into lintels
beside the shingly beach   over his shoulder
the ink drying slowly   whales on the sand
somewhere else and thick description
of the new everywhere tendrils   curving
across his page   all the children but one
on the ramble to the deserted bay
Hikutu eyes following   another historian
measuring footsteps over the hills   *vanished
to Hokianga* and the little rose hanging on
at the corner of the house   now you see me

but if you don't write it down
I will disappear   and if you squint
at the inscription without reading glasses
the wrong word will start down its road
a gambolling dog making for Great Exhibition Bay
wrong way wrong word wrong name
I saw something   he said in the land
waiting to invent its people

the dog led us to Oihi
and a pair of paradise ducks on guard
above the valley to the sea   there was a rose
where the rose had been torn out   shooting
green and defiant at the corner of wind
whacking the hillside   absolutely where they were
said the historian looking at our photos
and was there one by John King's grave
tiny pink flowers   no scent that I did smell
pūtangitangi wheeling overhead

fat buds appear on trees
as the rose dreams itself again
from cuttings on a windowsill   Mangungu
Ōhaeawai   coffee and muttonbirds at Te Corner
too late for The Trainspotter in Kawakawa
yes said the old rose grower's daughter
the council knows it's there   they invent
new reasons for cleaning up the reserve
and the historians keep bringing out
their boats and their books   they dip
their pens in black ink and draw parallels
across the pages and between the lines
a fig sucker at the pā site   an old lemon tree
in a fertile corner of land by the stream

degli angeli

I saw my angels   they were beautiful
beyond compare   flags snapping above the headland
combed blond by wind   they were sitting
each with disaster in a small pocket and they were
so beautiful in their resistance to the idea
of letting it fall into the world   they were meeting
in a room with light powered by small engines
perfect examples of resonance   and the distribution
of energy to this evolving flute   that tapering cup
in the hand of something like god   or the sound
of wind across hillsides   how to say it   they were
complete they were not defined they were still
and they were moving each moment   closer
to each other and further away   I saw them   they were
beautiful   they were the winds of heaven
in a small cup   unbreakable and looking at me

never dreaming

they came in a wave cloud   in bonnets
in gowns ballooned by the westerly flow
the slow circling of isobars   clockwise
counterclockwise   each with majuscule
definition   turning to the others
as sail pilots look for the marked channel
marvellous sarabande   starry gavotte
points on a map drawn by geometers
forgotten or disappearing into the beat
of a warm pulse   they call out
Dinah Elizabeth Hannah Jane   each of them
huge against the sky and turning around
to hook another's arm   Hannah Elizabeth
Dinah Jane   my daughters I left behind
will you forgive me   my sons I will bury
on the steep hillside   lend me grace
and a strong heart around the new house
sisters angels   clockwise and counterclockwise
we turn on our passage over the sea   behind us
the biggest iceberg yet to escape circumpolar
currents   ahead the three capes wrangling
beside us voices crying   Rina Heni
Irihapeti Hana   and our hands folded
carefully around the green shoots   sweet briar
crimson china   our undocumented fingers
weird with grief and the future   rose wreaths
floating with the tide on a harbour of jade
voices on the deck   playing draughts   playing
the governor   making a cartridge case
Rina Hana Heni Irihapeti   bring your feet

across the sky   looking back looking
ahead   makers of wreaths and small shrouds
ladies of the wind   come ashore
we have you almost at anchor again
almost between the heads and beating
into the westerly flow   fiducial angels
never dreaming where your names
will take you as the seas begin to rise

circadia

the dog is still imaginary   a space
without definition   each day is further
from the farewell and closer
to the black dots on the horizon
blindness: the movie is the title
of my next book   needing only time
to walk on water or buy the Nice
Feijoas that appeared yesterday
down the road   little Peace took me
four corners around the neighbourhood
a tank engine swerving to avoid
pavement tables   *Peace forward* I said
Peace right   this is not my dog
who is still imaginary   *Peace right*
the angels watching   holding their sides
Peace right   the four corners
marking out a lopsided rectangle
with wavy edges and stops for kerbs
Peace right   and we're under the trees
whose roots lift the asphalt   whose foliage
washes my face on wet mornings
she brings me to the house with rusted gutters
and peeling paint   we turn in under
the grandiflora   what else do you want to know
he asks me   then they're gone
sun and shade at the gate and two people
talking in the big room   you just know
one of them says   there is a dog-shaped space
the summer goes by with its tongue hanging out
an alphabet of dogs assembles around us

Gretel Haley Hugo Odette and now Orbit   flopped
at the feet of his minder who is collecting
for the annual appeal   his ears are soft
and just for one moment he fills
the dog-shaped space in our lives

heartland

white linen on the lawn
is moonlight and why didn't I know
we were sleeping out there last night
carried away in the same current
that will take us downriver this afternoon
green Tukituki waving tassels that whisper
Orepuki Hopupu ho nengenenge matangi rau
another river delivering words that run
from mountains to mouth   pulled from the knot
to join us out here on the lawn
in moonlight   where the garage sale was
but nothing sold so we moved
outside with the beds and the couches
hooked up the stove and some plumbing
and asked the neighbours in
the air is cool our thoughts deliberate
after the exertions of the day
a fishing camp and blue haze hanging
over the plain where cyclists sweat
the community triathlon in waves that pass
one two three   around the table at Terrace Road
with a bottle opener close at hand
copper silver and a redolent strip of blue
Tukituki   Tākitimu   whitebait fritters
next morning at the showgrounds   Tuahiwi
o te rangi moving to the horizon
from the lookout at Te Mata Peak
across the Hauraki where a black flag flies
and out to the coast at Miranda

ngā kaitiaki / the guardians

our mothers schedule another meeting
one from this side one from that
place where more things are visible
than we suppose   we've driven north
and Dallon's gallery is almost full
waves slapping under the floorboards
when you say your name our mothers
smile and it's boarding school in the war
and the same school thirty years later
you've come from Kashmir you've come
from Denmark you've come from Kaihū
from Kerikeri and Tauranga Bay
I am almost speechless and then I'm not
everyone in the room says their name
then we turn out the lights the better to hear
those Hokianga waves in the dark

a shell with a china handle
arrives in my hands   *demi-tasse*
he says and it's a coffee cup
from a small table under the painting
where Hagar wrestles with an angel
whale ivory for a bullwhip
he puts in my hands   the old house shakes
and the wind off the harbour remembers
who planted the date palm on the bank
where the path snakes down to the road
a double-hulled dinner plate
heavy in my hands   *rare as* he says
and we have three of them here   no bung

in the rim where the hot water went in
to keep the gravy warm
along the hallway he takes
a stick from the wall   my fingers
take in ivory and high polish   and then
carving that makes supplejack twists
below a cage of air
we follow him down   old tuatara
in hat and tails at his front gate   eyes closed
beside her whose eyes are open   who pours
coffee keeps dinners hot and holds it all
together   feathers brush her face
and the longtails whistle overhead

I take them their groceries he says
every three weeks   they're ninety they don't like
the city   still get up early four-thirty or five
drink date tea they make themselves
I don't like it   you know soak the dates in water
horrible stuff but that's what they do   ninety
I brought them down here for a holiday
three weeks and they worried so much   his dog
her chooks the garden the fishing   I had to take them back
we got to the bottom of the beach
and I gave him the wheel   he was like a kid
frightened hell out of us but I let him go
until we got to the stream then I took over
they were so excited the last few miles
I stayed up there with them   came back
with half the garden in Agee jars
and that smell of hot vinegar
among the tomatoes bubbling on the stove

land sea and sky

Lawrence Durrell arrives in Corfu
and sees the Pleiades in a pool of dark water
near the house he rents at Kalamai
under the glacid surface of the sea fishes
are moving like the suggestion of fishes
the Corfiotes indulge him and the rest
of the family when they get there   paradise
on earth and adjectives like stars
in his Mediterranean prose   he keeps faith
with the sisters in their misty pool
the colour of their eyes is everywhere
their seven songs reach through the years of war
and sad diasporas   and as he steps
ashore in Cyprus to begin Bitter Lemons
there they are   rising in a beautiful narrative
at Bellapaix for the beginning of summer
a world of water trims a world of fire   the map
on the bedroom floor survives the predations
of curiosity and terror   there they are
the flicker of their wings twinkling frostily
a flight of pigeons fanning out on the blue

a salute to the girls whose eyes
split the spectrum   *fire lion saffron*   and are
painted on narrow boats   *river ocean thunder*
making their way across the night sky
they learned to love the dark   they sprang
from doorways one bunch of ribbons
or the other in their excitable hands   look at this
they said and the warmth of one evening

or the coolness of another spread out
from the harbour entrance   girls how do you
split white light with terrestrial eyes
and where do you go when the door swings
wide   releasing you *ultra infra*
into a field of stars with names as strange
as your own   nobody ever explained
the jumps to left and right   the halos
of laughter they made   those girls my eyes

a new moon sits in the sky tonight
waiting for the sisters who are some distance
away *the suggestion of fishes* swimming
or flying like stars across the dark pool of the sky
up there it's summer and a girl brings cherries
to the surface in her lips as the poet watches
unable to believe his eyes   down here
winter and the heliacal rising of doves
on long strings that hold us to the earth
and one another as the little eyes open

the longest night

when John Donne writes *'Tis the year's*
midnight, and it is the day's, Lucy's, who scarce
seven hours herself unmasks   you need
the commas and the apostrophes to understand
the daze he's in as the planet hurtles
towards aphelion and all possessives leave us
out of pocket out of body out of mind
the very darkest night the black night the long night
of the poet's soul turned inside out   no hope
but Lucy whose name means light   who lost her eyes
in some terrible manner as saints do but is lucida
bright star and lucid in her seven hours of daylight
now also Lucina at midpoint above us   the half moon
that lights our midnight with trumpets and angels
if only John Donne would turn a little from his black fugue
and consider some of the other stories in the sky

when I asked Dave Eggleton about Matariki
he stayed up all night on the mountain Takarunga
measuring the luminosity of the city lights   listening
to the song of the container port cranes   he knew
what to do   *I lie on my back against the lip of the crater*
to gaze up like an anti-gravity bungee-jumper
at the star-trek of spaceship Earth   this midnight
brings visions to the poet in his observatory
he hears the hum of the volcano below him   he leaves
his body to fly over star mountains and he sees
eyes like paua lures in the star ocean   his long night
as an astral traveller returns him to Takarunga
when the sun comes up *orange as ripe persimmons*

in winter's leafless orchard   which is also the colour
of the car carrier he calls *a horizontal skyscraper*
gliding into the harbour as the city begins to wake

when Bradford Haami talks whales and stars
he uses his hands to mark out wide arcs that triangulate
the positions of travellers in space and time   this year
he's the resident writer on Takarunga and he knows
all about watching from the tops of hills for signs
of how the journey is taking its course   his hands fly
up and over 180°   *Puanga in the east at first light
Rehua in the west*   their child is the white-flowering
Puawānanga whose child is *Īnanga*   so get out the frypan
and plenty of butter   when the long vigil is done
the warm kitchen the steaming mugs of tea   these too
are part of the navigation we make through darkness
towards the breaking light of day   the stars go out
trailing clematis and running whitebait over the pale vault
where gold is chasing pink and silver to something
as deep as the ocean   from the abyss we come
through doorways that remain forever open

MANY HANDS

day one

barely there the water
that little boy went into the river
he was a monkey quite a monkey
he was a little boy he went out
the gate and didn't come back
grief from the long distance
dreaming him home

a face lit with words
she turns to me   ghost and the birds
singing in the dark as we leave
before sunrise   remember the shapes
of letters and write them quickly
singing birds in the dark   grief
to the dreaming mothers but singing
there is so much to do   Anna
Anna Maria   Anna Maria Dell'oso
silver grey maker
of tea and the distance
between two emphatic typewriters

ACQUIRING SATELLITES
ACQUIRING SATELLITES
PLEASE DRIVE TO THE HIGHLIGHTED ROUTE
PLEASE DRIVE TO THE HIGHLIGHTED ROUTE

hello Australia in the carpark
of Avis rentals where we're picking up
a red Mitsubishi   hello Karen
it's nice to be here it's nice to hear
your sweet voice attached

to the windscreen and telling us
how to get out of the airport the city how
to get on the road north   RECALCULATING
RECALCULATING   this is the Western
Distributor this is a ramp this is first left
second right enter roundabout and take
another look out the window   Karen baby
it's good to have you along on this side
of the water   hello to the brick veneer
to semis leaning in close in chorus
TRANSNATIONAL MOBILITY SISTERS
the highway opens its arms
the city falls behind   a speeding
red beetle on a moving map
ganglia more or less intact
more or less back on the ground

we're looking for the Putty Road
somewhere west of Windsor   galahs
crack up rosellas whistle   the day curves on and on
sulphur crests in a field hundreds of them
dead kangaroo dead kangaroo dead
kangaroo one big live one with balls
there he goes   unhurried ruminant
lolloping into the trees   what else?
Lola Ridge buried her mother
at Rookwood in August 1907
then left for San Francisco
how will we find her now?
three and a half stars at Singleton
on the New England Highway   out to it
cockatoo dreaming eating the miles
tearing centipedes out of the earth

day two

a Matilda tank in Matilda Place
gözleme for breakfast and oranges
from Bulga picked yesterday sweet as
sunlight on the edge of the oval
where two magpies are chasing off a crow
the little market has everything   country callers
in full swing   two cats named Strog
and Off   beef packs and canaries in a cage
we stock up on Pink Ladies and mandarins
and leave town with an old-time medley
on special today drifting from the rotunda

we bought a knife in Denman
to cut the Bulga oranges   we raced
a coal train and the valley fell away
in a green tilt that became a dividing
the dividing   The Great Dividing Range
hoopla! we listen to the frogs and parrots
of an unmarked stop beside the road
some hills some plains some cloud
some highway a bag of macadamias
the Ladies and the mandarins   life is good
and we've found the Blue Biddy
in Dunedoo right where Martin told us
it would be   a skinny breeze
information on a board and the train
departing with a lonesome whistle
in the early afternoon

what is a gramma?
and where is the rest of the solar system
on a scale of -38 million miles
if Neptune is here in Dunedoo
and the sun is an observatory dome
down the road in Siding Spring?

BLUE BIDDY	WHITE ROSE	BLACK SWAN
WHITE ROSE	BLACK SWAN	BLUE BIDDY
BLACK SWAN	BLUE BIDDY	WHITE ROSE

at the White Rose we order
ham sandwiches that come in perky triangles
with a doily underneath   we're washing
off the dust and making jukebox selections
when in walks Martin with the ghost
of Ludwig Becker who camped
with the supply party a long way west of here
as the Victorian Exploring Expedition
staggered towards oblivion   what Herr Becker
wouldn't have given for a bed at the Blue Biddy
a shower at the Black Swan or souvlaki
at the White Rose where Martin is asking
whether they should join us in the original décor
or take the smokers' seats outside
Becker opts for the street where he can observe
the utes with their roo bars and sketch
the delicate beauty of gum leaves
shingling in the wind   they're good companions
these two and it's with regret they part
near sunset   Becker for his dingy tent
Martin heading for the Golden Highway
that will swing him into another orbit

we watch them rolling away
and take a last look at outer space
for Dubbo on the Mitchell Highway
is where we roost tonight

day three

we are ten hours from Brisbane
says one source   but another *as the truck stops*
halfway to Broken Hill   the sun went down
behind the white bridge and the slow Macquarie
took another meander in its stride
how did we miss the billiard ball Pluto
on the roadside that's the ninth planet
in this drive-through solar system
where people make the difference?

LONGHAUL DRIVERS ARE SLEEPING
PLEASE CONSIDER THEM   DO NOT USE
ROOM TOWELS OR FACE WASHERS
TO CLEAN WINDSHIELDS   MIND YOUR HEAD
COMING UP AND GOING DOWN THE STAIRS

the crazy black and white bird
weep weep weeps somewhere in the trees
it's crisp and a long shadow slants
across one corner of this page   the windscreen
needs a wipe   Karen reiterates our position
but she's unreliable at this hour
so we take an independent route south
and east   fields of canola in flower

drive into our eyes and the plains are sprung
with morning *luteal and lovely*

tinka tinka tinka tinka
a teaspoon works its way across the room
at a hundred kilometres an hour
tinka tinka tinka tinka   furious tea
in the town on the old ten-dollar note
Henry Lawson has a museum here
and a statue in the municipal gardens
he's more famous than Lola
but they both grew up on goldfields
and knew how to stir up trouble
Henry lived in a North Sydney coffee palace
and drank at the Dawn and Dusk Club
did she?   we could ask the trainwreck
couple in the corner Miss Stirabout
and Herschel Bypass but they've disappeared
tinka tinka tinka on the wind
and a vacuum cleaner sucking up heritage
under the verandas in Gulgong

Mudgee is preservation houses
Rylstone at 47 Louee Street the gallery
where she is shorthanded but keeping it together
Rose how much are your biscuits?
your rhubarb chutney your lime and ginger
marmalade?   there is coal smoke
on the air in Lithgow   no network reception
and six nuns eating icecreams
in the carpark at McDonald's

we miss most of the scenic route
but make a perfect landing
at the corner of Wentworth and Hat Hill Road
the red-painted house the cream picket
hello hello hello   the door opens
it's Pam wondering where we've got to
and Jane out picking rhododendrons
teacups chutney marmalade and wine
begin the talk that catches its tail
and spins us round again   the gramma
is a pumpkin   the bird book shows us
willy wagtails red wattles white ibis
nankeen kestrels and magpie larks

day four

UP IN THE MOUNTAINS   UP IN THE MOUNTAINS
THERE YOU FEEL FREE   THERE YOU FEEL FREE

in 1836 Charles Darwin
lying on a sunny bank at Bathurst
sees a platypus with a rubbery bill
unlike those of the dried specimens
he is familiar with   the country is open
and rolling   the ants just as they are
at home on the other side of the world
falling into the ant-lion's conical trap
young Darwin has a moment of clarity
on the riverbank   there are two Creators
or One who nodded between labours
the platypus ducks and dives

in the water   a living non sequitur
they shoot it to get a closer look

we ramble up Wentworth Street
along Inconstant and back
through the Catholic Precinct
Pam explains how ghostly Sisters
walked the verandas of their retreat
and had to be persuaded to leave
there are tremors in the room
each night   nothing to worry about
the old house remembers its guests
a currawong *does that shrill thing
into pink air*   two kookaburras laugh
their heads off in the back garden
and there's a supply of tennis balls
for keeping off the cockatoos
the Brown Overarm the Zemiro Zap

at Govett's Leap we can hear
the waterfall and see the sulphur crests
floating over the trees below
at Leura there's an amphitheatre
of stone   an amphitheatre of soft light
on stone   an amphitheatre
soft sound of light on stone   a hillside
for jumping off   an opera for stars
in Katoomba we go to the Three Sisters
who may have been seven
if they are then we're here
looking up looking to the northeast
waiting for those tea lights to look down
and remember their breathing time

my friend you walk with me
up and down the stone steps
we are slow but we are here
late light on the cliffs   cold where
we stand at the edge looking over
behind us the sun going down
and the old rocks holding us up

on the news they're still talking
and the numbers haven't changed
73 72 4 1   the ungoverned
go about their business and fly
the skull and crossbones to mark
a line in the sand no prestidigitator
was expecting when the electorate
hung all of them out to dry

trains in the mountain passes
calling   rattling the window frames

day five

LET'S GO   LET'S GO NOW
LET'S GO TO THE CITY

where the poets are waiting
in their towers of shining glass
for the boxes of oranges we bring
from Narromine   for *the ruin of a sound*
as each word hits the air and bounces
LOVE DEATH AND THE WEATHER

flawless and funny   the streets are full
of advice for the cerebral hemispheres

⇐ LOOK LEFT   LOOK RIGHT ⇒
LOOK RIGHT ⇒   ⇐ LOOK LEFT

we got lost on Experiment Street
trying to drop off the ambrosia
we opened our ears and let the sounds
of a bridge roar through   every taxi
we took was driven by a poet
who had us down the moment we opened
our mouths   which island? my mother
my father my sister my cousin my aunt
twenty years five years a month last week
not Bauhaus but Powerhouse
a museum flicking past my inattentive ear
flip flop   an archipelago upside down in the sky
and Ken intoning Ken intoning stars
get in your eyes when you expect them least

or not at all   e toru ngā mea we sing
ngā mea nunui   three things and the most important
of these   ko te mea nui ko te aroha is love

poet you are	sitting there	sit
a small bird	bright-eyed	there
with a fierce grip	on life	bright
who knows	for one moment	eyes
what you think	make light	now
of this	poet	see
you don't let go	don't go	so
easily	just yet	far

there was the trip to Luna Park
and its big red maw   there were meetings
in coffee shops and full-day dérives
through second hand through reading rooms
through halls in which a hundred voices
rose and fell   profusion DE NOS JOURS
delirium DE NOS JOURS everything
DE NOS JOURS and no jour
too short to effect a sparkly rendezvous

she's up at dawn each day
to run with other poets of the metropolis
through parks and groves   along busy avenues
and across the harbour bridge
look right look left look out and about
poetic muscle working the urban grid

she watches someone climb over
iron gates that don't open until 7 am
he lopes off through the gardens
breath floating back on the dewy air
HE EAR ART HEAR T EAR
HEAR T EAR HE EAR ART

day six

the oranges are gone so we pack
the last of the ambrosia into bags and head
for Cockatoo Island   outside the fragrance
of fish sauce is overpowering and vendors
push handcarts piled high with teaspoons

buttons and clips for the families of dead soldiers
it's Legacy Day it's going gangbusters
with many hands to dig out an appellation
for this and other adventures we'd like to see
between our islands and their talking coasts
voters peons yahoos   café casino garage
reef riff roulette séance shipwreck wilderness
we're not going to solve it today and so
the expeditions take their leave of one another
promising to meet again one day soon

at the quay someone steps forward
with a talisman for the voyage   smooth in my hand
covered with bright trails and beating hearts   a stone
she calls caterpillar dreaming   a painted stone
from a place we can know nothing of   a gift to carry
to the island of abandoned industry redoubts
and cells for recalcitrants cut into the living rock
was there a fever hospital a dry dock a sail loft?
did the people of this place climb the hill
for eggs from the nests of these raging birds?
a libation in plastic glasses we make to them
the birds and the people   then the boat called
FRIENDSHIP floats us back in time to catch
the haka in front of a blow-up football
swaying gently beside the water

let's ride the monorail that tram
in the sky whose thunder reminds us
with pink and green cars that the Jetsons
will live forever   let's walk in the park
as the sun goes down and the bats begin
their hunt   memory reflects in a pool

with lights and a mausoleum   there's the hospital
the little pig with the golden snout
and water dripping from his bristly chin
there's the mint then the barracks that became
an asylum   there are the railings
and behind them the benches where one might sit
looking out at the balmy world
but your rules are the ravings of fevers
bred of shadows fantastic and vain
that are spun by the little white weavers
in the mystical loom of the brain
this is Lola 1906   she is good at reversing
the view and giving the silent a voice

at Mother Chu's we eat vegetarian
Peking duck and wonder about the wantons
crispy or with soup   delicious either way
the fishy pungence blanketing the city
has cleared off   we reach Macchiato
and get takeouts as rain begins to fall

little boar il porcellino
in your Florentine fountain pool
with frogs and turtles crabs and scallops
mustered at your feet   fresh water salt water
gift of a contessa little dribbling pig
whose nose we rubbed in the dark for luck
as memory unfolded contrejour against
the light of an Uffizi workroom   your silhouette
a restoration   a glimpse   another world

day seven

we're walking down Pitt Street
to meet her when the phone rings
in his pocket   there's been an earthquake
she says   a big one nobody dead but the city
on the plains is a mess   SMASHED   AFTERSHOCK
DOOMSDAY   SHATTERED BUT STOIC
headlines rumble as our calls queue up   jamming
the networks   *bricks became birds tiles turned*
to leaves and fell   they thought it was a rat a cat
a train   RŪAUMOKO ROCK AND ROLL
giving the chimney-pots wings

at the dance school by the harbour
where she brought her girls for years
on Saturday mornings we sit down
far away from the two typewriters hammering
the cold of that city on the plains
mama and papa are dead and their rings
are with the Madonna in the Abruzzo church
where it all began   the words tremble
under the weight they carry the distance between
the beginning and the end of this story   and others
we remodel as hours vanish and the tide
lifts boats outside the picture window

gales freshen   we stroll to Kirribilli
over the bridge and catch a water taxi back
to town   now it's time to visit 117 George Street
where the Académie Julian is in session
at the top of narrow wooden stairs   much as it was
when Lola Ridge was here   perhaps a student

perhaps a model for the life class perched on a stool
the premises have changed but the school persists
and it's easy to imagine her hauling canvases
or sketchbook from the ferry   mama and little son
awaiting her return each day to the North Shore
where she is shedding marriage and connections
to the mining town 1200 miles across the sea

her name is not part of the writers' walk
but Henry is there with many others as we enter
the Botanic Gardens looking for a man with a stone face
dappled by sunlight   finding instead Mrs Macquarie's Folly
ibis on patrol and a faun with the face of someone
who fell off the Manly ferry and drowned
in the long distance between periphery and home
here McCahon went on his all-night walk
with the spirits whose images in the rock beneath
his feet are tracks of light for the dispossessed
the deranged the lost and the breathing dead

p e r i p h e r y   the golden limousines
of wedding parties circle park and gardens   the bride's
feet are sore but her girls have taken off their shoes
as they troop back from the fountain   did they pose
by Diana and her dogs or drink from a spouting turtle?
our dreams tonight are transfers from TV
sand volcanos in the bathroom rivers of mud where
we want to drive the car nine people dead
in a plane crash at Franz Josef   *(don't you remember?*
won't the lost shake for any cry at all?)   we wake
in the dark to get an airport shuttle   out on the street
the sun is coming up and the ground is still   four girls
in short skirts and high heels petition a driver

but he won't take them three blocks to their hotel
so off they go   a little the worse for wear but clearly
crispy wantons leaving their wedded sisters now
for embarkation to a palace among the stars

THE MEZZALUNA ROCKING

the digger and the faun

Joe Lynch is that you   the untidy
soldier above the eighty-six names
of those who didn't come back   you've
removed your hat   you stare down
the road to where the Kea is embarking
another load of partygoers for the city
Joe Lynch your blue eyes are entirely notional
but he hears the quartermaster's whistle
and remembers the boats taking them off
under cover of darkness   did he set you up
little brother   a paid job after the war
before you ran for the Sydney boat
the mad Lynches leaving town together

it wasn't the first time   and maybe
he wanted the face of a returned man
up there on the stone that faces
the harbour   you were both on the turps
in King Street by the time they unveiled it
celebrating another adventure with
the art-loving public   goatfoot dancer
redheaded slinger of mud and one-liners
Joe Lynch you roaring Dionysian   quiet
in bronze above another harbour   watching
the ferries plug around the point   they said
you jumped off because the Kiandra was slow
and the bottles in your pockets heavy
they said you wanted to get to the party
Joe Lynch is that you   digger and faun
watching each other across the dark water

after the war

an army whistle   but not
the one my grandfather had at Gallipoli
because J Hudson and Co of Birmingham
whistle makers since 1880   have stamped it
1916 and my grandfather   now in France
and not wanting to lose it   scratches his name
on one side before attaching the lanyard
to the breast pocket of his tunic   probably not
the one in the photograph where he holds
a riding crop in his intact left hand and is
combed and clean   a studio in Cairo perhaps
before they got to the Dardanelles
his Acme Thunderer drilling precise holes
in the desert air of the Protectorate

the whistle came back with him   my mother
remembers her mother using it to call them in
at bedtime and for dinner at midday   children
whistled under the mountain that took each of them back
children who whistled their children to the same
starting line and then watched them disperse   taking
the carved chair the camphor chest the portrait
of the dead first child   and the whistle   emblems
the young man made or took for his own
after the war   my grandmother listed telegrams
cards letters of condolence then destroyed
or put aside the wedding photo   we never saw it
and surely there was one   31 August 1920
peacetime taking hold and maybe a honeymoon

my mother remembers also how he took
her mother on a trip to the Dutch East Indies
leaving the business and the children
in the care of others   bringing back
the Bali doll the carved coconut shell ornaments
the chest with its whirling horsemen
two swords from Java   ceremonial but still sharp
and the photos that betray the memoirist writing
each day in her book of luncheon and the Javanese
bringing bananas to the quay   of the temple at Borobodur
and natives at Lake Leles   Mrs Pizzy   Mr and Mrs Jonas
We'll remember this charming meeting in Banyuwangi
always   on the back of the KPM menu card

Holystoning the deck   Captain Stahl and his son John
Tea plantations   Quinine plantations   Chinese gardens
Singapore   Port Moresby   Saigon   Port Vila   Denpasar
Pounding rice   Bullfight   Funeral pyre   Native dances
Health and wealth and happiness   Ever friends
7 September 1939   her face is strained
under the shady white hat but she never liked
having her picture taken and nobody talked then
about hysterectomy though my mother is sure
this is why they went   a grand tour not too far
from home because anyone could see
there was going to be another war   no photo
of the ship in the Rangitoto Channel this morning
13 October 1939   48 passengers 500 tons of cargo
the doll the chest the swords the delicate carving
he understood   the wife and children he did not
MAETSUYCKER HOLLAND   huge letters
on both sides of their great white yacht
tricolours of the Netherlands painted on her bows
a white ship steaming up the channel

harbour lights

my father's blue eyes   shining
with tears he won't admit to   and which
we can't see up here on the afterdeck
of the Picton ferry   he is looking up   waving
from the wharf   we are waving back and calling
though we know he can't hear us   all day
we drove to catch the ferry that is taking us
away   he got us there in the nick of time
triumphant now as the boat pulls out   green water
between us   up here   and down there
he waits until he can't see us any longer
then tangles with rush-hour traffic
on the motorway north   two semis give him
trouble but he pushes on   a cup of tea
at Levin then the four hours to home
a long day   when the Valiant pulls in
my mother gets up and they talk into the night
drinking cocoa   we're over the strait and safe
in the next house on the journey to Canada   but
I remember my father's blue eyes and the tears
we couldn't see against the late sun   my father
driving north as we sailed south   the last time
I saw him   his blue eyes full of tears

lomu

and now the other black dog
grinning and wagging   bat ears hoisted
nose to the wind   eater of gravy-soaked
tea towels   pie thief rabbit digger   co-pilot
riding shotgun in all the vehicles   deaf mute
weight on all the beds   now the black dog
sleeps under the avocado at Weld Road
wrapped in an old blanket and keeping an eye
on the three pigs' ears luck has brought
his way   now the black dog sleeps

olive

the day of the explosion they postpone
her arrival   two men walk out and agony
begins its clinch   we crouch by the radio
unable to help   thinking *they could all be dead*
hoping for a miracle twenty-nine times
the size of a mountain in the eye of a needle
stitching blue heaven to green earth
let them walk out let them walk out alive

it is too dangerous   when they bring
her at last three days have gone by   each
more terrible than the one before   angels
look out of the eyes of this dog who is here
because I am blind and the world is huge
with possibility   we walk her in a raw wind
not knowing we shouldn't   a mistake
that costs but is not the end of the world
under the dark mountain of sorrow

when they show the dust blasting
out of the portal for fifty seconds   we know
there is no hope but listen as machines prepare
to enter the shaft   today I learned how to comb
how to check ears eyes nose teeth and all over
for the baseline that is hands on a warm body

when the drill breaks through   the images
show that nobody reached the oxygen refuge
when they find a cap lamp still flickering
in the camera's eye four and a half days

and a kilometre in   we go out for the first time
just around the block   only to hear
there's been another explosion

dog   I hold my breath as you take us
into the world I can't see   each day
a little further a little more command a little
sliver of hope under the dark mountain
where fear waits with its next fuse
and rescue is unlikely any time soon

from all over the world gear and advice
pours in   a third explosion sets the coal burning
deep underground   *the trapped miners*
become *the lost men*   *the men who lost their lives*
and finally *the entombed men*   now they gag the mine
starving the fire of oxygen and the violent language
of despair cries out upon us   threading the path
between light and darkness pain and rage
care and the undoing of everything we cared for

my dog how can you move with such grace
through these days   pulling sea and sky along
with you under the red-flowering trees   mixing it
up and down the road with all comers   this is not peace
but motion   ten thousand people looking up
the valley to a dip in the ranges while someone sings
You'll Never Walk Alone   not peace but motion
what is her name they ask me and I say
she has been here since the start   her name is Olive

honey meadow

what do we know about her   only
that she was in these places   Clare Castle
1835 Hereford 1837 Gloucester 1838
and 1839 Clonmel 1840 Leeds 1842 Doncaster
1843 St John's 1845   these are the births
we have found   but of her   nothing
his armful of lilies   a girl turning back to look
at one who can't see   a voice in the dark
singing to the first baby wrapped in a summer shawl
and to the last   as the bright leaves fell
on Newfoundland stone   and the ships
that would take all of them home   and beyond
swung at anchor in Avalon   lamenting
her disappearance   the hem of a skirt
her warm arms and that clear voice   let them fly
my babes   let them fly over the ocean   let them
find happiness in the bright world   a blue stone
I put into each small hand   and this song
of the summer place and the snow blanket
the end wrapped around the beginning
and footsteps gone far away from me

dear sister anne

I write at the first possible moment
from the place we have come to   knowing
you will be anxious to hear and the news
so long getting there   a ship leaves
tomorrow on the evening tide so I have
this passage of hours snatched from sleep
in which to scribble and weep a few wet drops
but not on my words or they will be spoilt and nobody
the wiser about our adventures

darling the boat was a murder
though I must smile and say it was nothing
out of the ordinary   the world turned
upside down and beloved faces veiled
behind ocean spray   you won't remember
the voyage from Halifax but mama's white face
haunts me still and the rocking of a boat
is the rocking of a dark cradle in my brain

it was long ago   and this voyage
ended with shouts of joy from the quay
as the Grahams spied us being brought off
and were round us in an instant   children dogs
bags hullabaloo of sister falling into brother's arms
my Lewis teasing tall nephews with tears
running down his cheeks   they have named
the baby after me which is an honour
and a delight   she runs to meet us calling
for a kiss a song a story from over the sea

we are staying with John and Sophia
and already there is talk of buying land
adjacent to theirs in this perch above the town
and going into business together
there are folk who will pay and well
for the green-fingered touch of the Carrells
meanwhile gardens burst with early summer
new potatoes sugarsnap peas fat strawberries
each day for the table   I wish you could see us
feasting after the months of salt beef and biscuit

three icebergs we saw in the southern ocean
each one afloat on the deep past   summer in
St John's when you were a baby we counted
white castles drifting outside the harbour mouth
and filled them with splendid dreams   they say
we have come far enough south to see the aurora
and that it holds a singular beauty   dear sister
I will lift my eyes to the great darkness beyond
this hillside   and when I find curtains of light
shimmering gold blue purple orange and green
I will know you are watching from your high place
among the ceaseless artistries in circumstance

jackson's road

I am twenty-four   a labourer
well used to moving about   I liked
the Greyhound from the moment I saw her
in the fog at Gravesend   when we started
down the river I did not look back   everything
points south   we will eat up the latitudes to zero
then reel them out day by day   she is a true clipper
American-built for the passenger trade   chartered
this run for Port Cooper and loaded three feet deeper
than usual   the light chariot turned heavy wagon
says her master but still calculates 100 days
port to port   if the winds hold plain sailing

I got my kit organised and fell in
with the mess mates assigned to this corner
of the compartment   our cooking is fair
our cleaning exemplary but for others passing
up and down the forward hatch for water and coal
they keep us busy and forfend boredom   the chaplain
holds school on deck most days to which I go for exercise
of mind and access to ink and paper   evenings we tease
the doctor with forays to that quarter of the deck
reserved for the single girls   a fine correspondence
has ensued in the columns of the Daily Record
puffing of abominable pipes   flounce of petticoat virtue
the timbers shake to an old two-step
oak and locust wood   honey and pearl

new constellations rise out of the sea
the Dove the Triangle the Peacock   hull and sail
of the ship Argo the Cross and its Pointers
a reverend gentleman takes us east to west
his arms describing arcs that join up magnitudes
and rearrange the polar carousel   on one side
of the page I trace the star canopy as best I can
on the other I plot the daily coordinates of our course
against the schoolboy map I measured off by degrees
we are a series of dots looping the Atlantics
to the Roaring Forties   along the way
I have marked the islands we saw   St Antonio
Tristan da Cunha Inaccessible Nightingale
Hog Penguin Apostle and Possession

we are nearly at the longitude of the Snares
and have three or four days to run northeast
before finding Lyttelton   I fold away the map
with its almost complete necklace of ink and pencil
and imagine myself on Monday afternoon
walking up the road to my sister's house

frederick walter

brother William sister Dorrie   your persuasions
and my savings shake hands over a passage to this
far country and I follow you   working on farms
and the railroad   Timaru Hornby Tinwald Burwood
then we were up Dannevirke way and the boys went
droving or milking until the war came along   Kumeroa
Whanawhana Opeke Downs   little places they exchanged
for battlefields then hospitals   all shadow names
to William's brood and to the gardener Carrells

how does it go   a Carrell girl
married a Graham and out they came   two Carrell brothers
followed their sister   one Carrell wife called two brothers
to Lyttelton   one of them married a Graham daughter
named for his sister   then we all spread out
and had big families   kept in touch when the wives
liked each other and through a string of childless
first daughters   sister Dorcas brother William   between
us we are the plains the city the scrub land
the garden the store the works and the railways
laid in the ground or whirled on the Lord's high wind

I am a devout man   twenty-three years
in the congregation at St John's Latimer Square
then I was away from town and my Dorrie with me
under the stone in Burwood   looking east to the sea
and south to the hills where we began   brother William
sister Dorcas   we are invisible to our descendants
who cannot piece out the resemblances we carry
or say why our mother's name appears in one family

but not in another   I pay it no mind
being but a name on an old stone   waked up this day
when the earth rumbled and boulders as big
as houses came walloping down the hills   brother William
sister Dorrie   I imagine you climbing unsteadily
from your open tombs in prospect of glory and with trembling
hearts   surely it is the day of reckoning   surely
we are broken into the Lord's judgement
children crying as the shaking begins again
outstretched hands transparent against the Light
bootless feet set down in the swirling Flood

experiments (our life together)

here is my experiment with the dark

we run to the top of the street and crossing it
become aware of the fountain's lip and mosaics
under water pink blue hyaline we step through
the foot bath yes the gold leaf is holding on

here is my experiment with stars

it is a dormitory on the top floor this two o'clock
the babies wrapped loosely in sheets asleep
and somehow not falling out of their little moulded beds
the blinds drawn down the afternoon heat

here is my experiment with humours

aqueous the home movie
tears on the lens and always the return
to rivers their flumes and fumaroles
so plural so carrying so carried away

here is my experiment with light

which leaves me now the dear shapes
gone to sound the end wrapped around
the beginning a piano in a dark room that is
quite what it is like and never the same

here is my experiment with river

memory and the wind ruffles her hair
there are no fences on the sun only a truck
bouncing on the flood its wheels gone and us inside
scared to death and still steering

here is my experiment with rain

we swim and let the current take us
where it will which is some toehold around
the corner under cliffs of black honeycomb
the saltwater pool afloat on its concrete rim

here is my experiment with amygdala

in the morning we find a bar and marmellata
as the sun comes up and the streets are cool
a slice of duomo at the end of each stony block
an orchestration a theatre of the mind

here is my experiment with immanence

who was waiting there who was asking me
to look at heaven from the end of a dark wharf
and when I did when I raised my empty eyes
the city was there a necklace of light a horizon

here is my experiment with periphery

who was asking me not to forget
rippling scales in another room a gallery
at the top of the stairs a cupola a vault
a canopy a river of light on the ceiling

talking to the sky

here I give up the supplicant

who followed me around with legs
like uncooked pasta the fresh sort that folds
over itself in the sealed packet and you toss it
in handfuls to the salty boiling water

here I give up the rosicrucian

I could have been if things had been
different on the backstreets of Paris when
mama danced and papa played a violin
three-quarters the size of the hat I wore then

here I give up the detail

I saw with my own eyes the earth's shadow
eating up the moon going down on the western rim
blood red or pitch black because of the ash cloud
padam padam padam we will fly low today

here I give up another ghost

who rolled the umbrellas and laid them end
to end at the foot of the bed a peace offering
already too late the big diesels in reverse not
this channel but the other one between islands

here I give up my old right eye

and set out for Jerusalem walking on my
hands for amusement and having no need
I let them go bouncing on ahead out of pocket
released back into the joyous microwave

here I give up my good left eye

from the waterline she has made a coast
stretched out in epithelial layers dark plantations
here and there a dip in the dunes she is pleased
with and waves rolling towards the vacated beach

here I give up my hand in front of my face

she was there yesterday but now she is gone
lifted into the plane of hand-coloured lace
her smile her green eyes her lily of the valley
bouquet the first day of spring and forever

here I give up false security

think of it our tender feet engaging each day
with the shaky surface we depend on forgetting
it is a boat forgetting it is a slippy fish there are
bumps and plumes and today we will not fly

here I give up the red flash

fovea holding out against expectations a dip
on which to focus perhaps the entrance to a valley
where we will go one day walking upstream to some
bright source in the hills behind Ascension

a brief history of time

the book slips past my ears
on the flight over   three hours
following the sun folding up corporeal
reality and I'm not finished as we begin
the descent into   earlier   tray tables
secured seats in the upright position   not
a molecule lighter or less perturbed
than the cold air under our wings   we step
back in the same day and forget an hour
the spooling voice entered and can't leave
or leaves many times without us   going on
split or spilt from departures arrivals terminals
the book slips by and I am not done

she came out of the crowd a stranger
leaving the city we were entering   please take
this she said   it's good for seven days   but
the metcard she gives me expired yesterday
a platform is a crossing place   alight depart
the gift of a stranger is not always legible

in one glissade we see the waiter in his brocade
waistcoat through the glass at Grossi   his brother
tall and dark walking into Self Preservation   their cousin
on her way to work at European around the corner
where we sit outside in the sun and wind with balloon
hearts waving foolishly over our heads   listening
to the lived detail the trail that will take us from Cumulus
to Gingerboy Sichuan House to Saint Ali's Journal to

Auction Rooms My Sister Says Il Fornaio Brunetti Bar Fred
and phone-ins from places under consideration or just off
the map they draw for us and change a moment later

the young people into whose lives we have tumbled
whose city we enter with passports that declare distance
even as we close our arms around them   the young people
we were in another life without trepidation and full of bounce
darlings beware be happy and beware   look after each other
your voices once more in our ears your heads bent over
another app another cloud another touch pad   there's a tram
in two minutes ten minutes twelve minutes to take us home
across the dark river on a freezing night in July

a little earthquake on the platform at Princes Bridge
to match the shiver underfoot in Auckland the night
we were packing   shadows at Alimentari   the zip my fingers
could not learn   the forest of misery on the walls
around us   rain and sun a monkey's wedding   a book
or a tram slipping by with that sweet shifted clang sampled
from ancestral bells and played through a speaker
the young man in the park with his head in his hands
the young woman adrift   running down Collins Street
with Charles Buckmaster   the voice of Lydia Valerio
leaving Torino di Sangro oh mother I don't know where
I'm going   for a flat above a tyre shop in Collingwood   or who
I'll meet when I get there   the Eureka stockade thrown
ninety floors into the sky running red lines under our feet
rumbling bass surplus to requirements real or imagined
and people in a glass box moving out from the side of the tower
darkened walls made suddenly translucent   the sound
of shattering glass   who cleans these windows anyway

we fill a big table here a small table somewhere else
jumping from story to story   who could remember it all
the soundshell the lovers by the fountain the pigeonnier
the observatory the winding stair the view due north
to that other shrine of remembrance and its magnolia path
above the Sangro   we sit with our children who are meeting
each other for the first time   a confusion of pronouns
perfectly clear at the table which gathers but does not snap
the collation   the collection   the warm collocation
now drifting to its next appointments   à bientôt à bientôt

à bientôt   till Friday till Thursday till tonight
the swan-necked decanter the quiet dog creeping
onto a friendly knee by the fire   the mezzaluna
rocking out along the bay or through the fine crust
pulled from the hot oven   the mezzaluna of doubt
of two hands of cutting it fine   as the doors close
the bell clangs and the drunk begins his hyena call
to the black universe then charms a small boy in a paper hat
it's my birthday too very same as yours same as you   I am
going to see my friends all my friends tonight   seven days
of crossings going off like steel drums   again and again
we say goodbye and walk into Hill of Content where the book
opens itself to the very page I was on   real or imagined
starting over on the way back against the turn of the earth

SOME DAY

earthwalker

I set out again in the morning of the world
moving south the mountain behind   but never
out of sight   aroha-pai I said to my mother
and sister   don't cry   this is something
I want to do   catch the skein of stars behind
the mountain   pull its snow blanket close
in the snapping blue air   black maire
under my fingers and the blade looking for
roads that will shape what I cannot say
now or perhaps ever   the mountain hooks
my heart the wood my dreams   at Ngaere
the lake and its trees flick past and are gone
here the mountain paused to weep   I move south
putting summer and her face behind me
aroha-pai   I have forgotten the tiny figures
we made in the snow cup of the crater
the day of the open climb   but I have not
forgotten the curve of the maire   I have not forgotten
the stars setting over the mountain and the cold
leave-taking as our train pulled into the station

awapuni

when the horses were drawn up
we became a host   silks across the moon
were not more beautiful than our eyes
straining to make out a winner   a loser
at the edge of the track   a path to undying
on the boisterous roar of the crowd

arrower

we stand in the stream a second time
Psyche and Philomel with us   but now also
Minotaur and Ibuki   Maunganui   Hawkes Bay
Star of India   Limerick   Tahiti   Arawa   Athenic
Orari   Ruapehu   Waimana   we clear the straits
and Minotaur takes the lead   Ibuki
the right flank   Psyche the rear   Philomel
the left flank   between them the transports
form two lines   Arawa leading to port   Maunganui
to starboard   eight cable lengths apart
in perfect weather we turn west   I am part
of an intention   an arrow laid on the sea
face to the sky and wrapped in a blanket
I stay on deck when the boat begins to roll
sick like everyone else the first two days
I keep one eye on the horizon   marking
troughs and crests in the grain   we greet
whales and porpoises   we march around
Hobart   apples and flowers from the crowd
pick up Pyramus and the Australians
at Albany and turn north   floating palaces
of light on dark water   before the blackout
before Cocos and Colombo   before Aden
and Suez   in single file we pass through
the canal   guns and searchlights ready
to take on the Arabian moonlight

zeitoun

the mirror image the second self the place
of olives remembered in a famous seaport
called also Peace by Farsi speakers   in Fujian
where the silk road begins   the guidebook
is unequivocal   each sits in the shade
of the other offering a long view   almost
I make out the dense pattern of sails
almost the exchange of hostilities   and trade
in the souk then as now   bolts of satin
flying fish shimmering in the morning sun

horseman

we always had ponies   mostly fat
and happy to have four at a time kicking
along to the river pool   later on there were
picnics hay rides and family excursions
to Dawson Falls Mangamahoe or   once
the Meeting of the Waters   we swim the horses
in the Nile below the Delta barrage   trek sometimes
between date palms and lush berseem   but desert
sweat coated with grey dust is our signature here
the khamsin blows   a cloud of black locusts
strips the small farms bare   we fight our way
back to camp through dummy lines
buy oranges in the desert and talk of France

ismailia square

I went back again and again
great banks of purple bougainvillea
but I couldn't find that room   I saw
arching over the road the doorway
sandals of gold toe-caps of gold
I passed through into a workroom
beaten gold inlaid with lapis
and there she was   not very tall
a walking figure with the head
of a dog   straight shoulders
and blue eyes fixed on the void

foot soldier

a jam tin bomb I give to you
wrapped in a Turkish sock   dead boots
sticking out of the fresh sap wall
bits of shattered mirror for periscopes
heat and flies and putrefaction   words cover
wounds and decomposing flesh   two pints
of water is better than no water at all   night bathing
with bullets mule carcases and ship's fuel
beats washing in a tin cup up on the ridge   Imbros
and Samothrace float on the cloudless blue
beyond the blockade and the white hospital ships
another world   when they call an armistice
we form up in burial parties and spend the day
digging stacking collecting our dead and theirs
piles of bodies and weapons at the centre line
drawn between us   then back to the trenches
at 5 pm and there we were in hell again   digging
and fighting   digging and dragging and fighting
the wounded haunt my waking   the dead
my sleep   a terroir of exorbitance and depletion
in Shrapnel Gully   sitting in an armchair
washed ashore with other wreckage   I fish out
a postcard of Heliopolis and write   *heartily delighted*
with your Trinity College results   we are enjoying
splendid weather & having a swell time
this ought to make a splendid tourist resort
later on but if you come right away bring a gun

ari burnu

from the arm of the chair I remove
a single lath   split by sun and rain
but serviceable   the tree fern I carve
bends over notched hills and a bird
underneath I scratch AKE AKE KIA KAHA
and take it up the beach to put on the grave
of Manny Marfell   who knew the back country
better than any of us   and won't be
going home to his rough and tumble life

night fighter

eight inches square the white patches we sew
on the backs of our shirts   no coats no blankets
no lights no cartridges   just bombs and bayonets
up the side of the Dere in the dark   the destroyer
turns off her searchlight at 10 pm and stops pounding
the position on that crazy overhang   we pitch on up
into their lines   take the top and hold on
a day and another night   to be sent forward
into the trap that waits below the crest
of Chunuk Bair   as the sky lightens they come
for us again   ALLAH ALLAH ALLAH
faster than a galloper louder than death   our white
patches fall off and we are finished with the place
I remember   stretchering all day to the beach
one hand tied up in a dirty bandage   the steady beat
of engines taking us off under cover of darkness

reigate

after the hospital English trees   and furlough
among strangers who never left home   but look
like all of us   they are kind and take photographs
on the lawn at tea and on the terrace   they want
to make up for the bad blood   the melancholia
hanging around uncertain smiles   the snap
we take on the balcony outside his room in autumn
sunlight   one in uniform and still banged up
the other about to sit finals and become
a Fellow of the Royal College of Surgeons
I know you will be delighted with this   he writes
for never have we been taken together before

bombardier

the doglegs that took us from Sling
to Alexandria   Mosca to Marseilles
slow entrainment through spring and all
its blossoming orchards orderly vineyards
clustering villages busy towns   to Le Havre
where we taught ourselves gunnery and supply
to Armentières which taught us   nothing
we didn't already know   three blasts
on the whistle send us diving for cover
little sister   as the plane pokes around
taking photographs that could give away
the guns behind a factory door   or a wall
in someone's back garden   inky dinky
parlez vous   the estaminets are full
little sister   old men and boys dot the fields
bringing in a harvest where there is one
we go south in easy stages   St Omer to Langpré
les Corps Saints   Amiens to Bonnay and Corbie
summer is gone and we have come to the valley
of the Somme   our gun carriages
founder the horses starve   we pack gas shells
to forward pits and watch the first line of tanks
lumber off behind curtains of accurate fire   little sister
there is language for this   and for everything else
we fall into knock down break up dig out push away
there is language for everything but the cost is
unspeakable   I was there I did these things
for fifty-two days then we were taken out
and sent to Fleurbaix with what was left
little sister   inky dinky parlez vous en

caterpillar valley

in the dead hour he comes
from the Casualty Clearing Station
at Gezaincourt   such a pretty name
if we had ears to hear it   we talk
such a long time we talk   he is
a tourniquet a suture a hollow needle
I am trebuchet bombarde heavy mortar
between us file columns of men poisoned
by gas   bandaged eyes   one hand
on the shoulder of the man in front
they shuffle past the little cemetery

quartermaster

each footprint draws the eye of a searching gun
knee-deep in snow we walk backwards
with feather dusters   covering our tracks
more or less   spreading big white sheets
in front of our own guns after firing
to conceal the fan-shaped marks in the snow
leather and sheepskin waistcoats   whale oil
for sick feet   new diagnoses for sick souls
the hard frost   the hard frost
our mother in stocking feet outside the window
listening for the baby's cry in the dark   trying
to remember how many cartridges have been fired
from the gun in the dead drunk grasp of him
who torments her   our father   who shot
at the six-year-old then at her and now lies
dead to the world in bed with the four children
she walks to the next farm and raises the alarm
she will press charges she will not take him back
kicked in the head by a horse when young or not
cut feet and terrified heart   the mountain
standing silver ghost to her trail of tears
our mother before we were born   of whom
he could say when they came to wake him
she might have kept it quiet   the guns put down
successive lifts   wheel to wheel
in the only available cover

te henui

she takes a spade and digs
them in side by side   black earth
to the chin then under they go
looking sideways at each other
the one they lost to the river
the other to unspecified illness
two small boys   our brothers
whose names she repeated
in our names   calling you
by the drowned one's name
calling me always by the other

undertaker

it was too much for you   when we were
mining at Messines you were neurasthenic
in Brockenhurst   then in charge of invalids
on Ionic returning home as we drove deeper
into the Ypres salient   coming to the place
called Passchendaele I called out your name
but you did not hear and so we went on
weary and heartsick   we crossed
somewhere in the Indian Ocean   two
dazzle-painted ships with their cargoes
of hope and despair   you were gone
in and out of the hospitals trying to work
with torn wings and the shame   unable
to explain why you couldn't come back
I set up the business again   breathed
hot wood and the sweet scents of
the machine shop   trying to forget
your shaking hands trying to imagine
a pathway that might bring you home
it was no good   when you lay down
in the leaves of the forest with morphia
running softly along such ragged
highways as were left to you that night
I was dreaming of the cone rising
out of the bight   blue with distance
my brother of whom we will not speak
your children will grow up with excised
details   your sweet Madeline will struggle
to understand why you ran away
my brother face to the stars and voyaging
over the endless shoulder of the mountain
how is a bird   where is spring   ake ake ake

kopuatama

where else would I lie   having brought
so many others to the place   stood by
the open grave   riroriro threading
its song with the grief of snuffling relatives
then driven the back roads foot to the floor
thrashing the big car and singing at the tops
of our voices Some Day When I'm Awfully Low
the way we might have done on a different
road in the springtime just around the corner

WIND AND WEATHER

the telegram arrives and sets in motion
an ordered chaos   someone to help Maggie
with the little ones and bring them to meet
the Tuesday boat   decent dark but no need
for ribbons or armbands   a rain of sympathy
trooping through the front door   the house fills up
with scones and damp handkerchiefs
arrangements are made   tickets bought   bags packed
I have the black dress but I will not wear it   enough time
for that   the eldest eighteen the youngest two   seven lives
seven sets of eyes asking   what happened   how could he
leave us like that   one howls one sulks one turns away
they reproach me and I have no answer   Tuesday perhaps
the cold and the rain   the breakwater under lights
loading late cargo   ten o'clock before we leave
and the dark wraps itself around my aching head

dream of three graces coming ashore   dream
of their white arms and laughter diving headlong
into the shallows   dream of geese or swans
dream of spray   of courtship   of Isabella dresses
caught with child   dream of Canada   dream
of Lachine   dream of oceans rapids graces
an orchard in summer   an orchard in fall
cotton print eider down you have swept me
away   dream of racehorses and gunpowder
fire at sea fire on the mountain   dream of three
graces coming ashore   dream of a silken shallop

By telegraph today, 9 a.m. New Plymouth S.E., gale, overcast, gloomy, sea considerable swell. Manukau Heads N.E., strong breeze, overcast, bar smooth. Auckland N.N.E., fresh breeze, cloudy. Napier N.E., fresh breeze, overcast, sea slight swell. Wellington N., light breeze, cloudy. Cape Farewell N.N.E., fresh breeze, overcast, raining, sea heavy. Lyttelton S.E., breeze, blue sky. Port Chalmers Calm, foggy. Bluff Calm, clouds passing.

he is a good boy and brings us tea
at first light   the storm falls away
and we go on deck to watch the sunrise
shivering and muffled to the eyes   together
at the rail   my tall son who knows how
to be silent   does he remember the courtroom
the chair they stood him on to swear on the book
to tell the truth   that his papa fired the gun at him
and at his mama   that he missed and she ran out
of the house   that he slept on the sofa in the kitchen
when his papa was home   that he walked by himself
to the big bed when the light went out   does he
remember how they patted his head and threw out
the case   how twelve men looked the judge in the eye
and swallowed a version of events that would bring him
home   cautioned only against excessive drinking
because we needed him and they knew it   remortgaged
the farm that same morning and we stumbled on
a while longer   does he remember does he remember
the truth or the stories we told   the sun breaks through
low cloud   mother he says   you are crying

suddenly we arrive at Huia talking
high tide and there is almost no beach
a line of fish skeletons at our feet
a party trapped on rocks nearby calling
for help   faintly and we don't hear them
gazing out across slick water to the Heads
it's Saturday   willows whiten aspens quiver
little breezes dusk and shiver   a line of
fishbones and danger   the signal station
with its armful of flags the little steamer
through the wave that runs forever   over
the bar   he taught her and she taught me
recitation in a choir of breakers   by the island
in the river   a harbour now and a voice

By telegraph today, 9 a.m. New Plymouth Calm, blue sky, sea rough. Manukau Heads N.W., light breeze, gloomy, bar smooth. Auckland N.W., light breeze, clouds passing. Napier Calm, blue sky, sea smooth. Wellington N.E., light breeze, overcast. Cape Farewell N.W., light breeze, overcast, sea moderate. Lyttelton Calm, overcast, gloomy. Port Chalmers S.W., cloudy. Bluff N., breeze, cloudy.

two young lovers lately wed   words bounce
off the wharf pilings   dangerous and beautiful
we went to Toronto who knows why   his laughing
eyes the adventure Lizzie you are getting round
he said and we went back with our piece of paper
to run to the end of the world together   the child
born three days off the ship and off he went to find us
a home   words bounce   we are here again
tying up to the wharf Lizzie you will love the place
plumes and lights and music   the harbour
to which I come now the ferry across   two hills
and between them the house to which I come now
black skirts brushing grown child   bone weary
in the soft September night   young lovers fled
away and rough hinterlands between
I come back to the place where we started
finding him in the front room with snowdrops
murmur of receding voices   new wood

a body on the beach early morning light   a body
on the beach washed up by the talking waves
a body on the beach by the ferry wharf   a body
on the sand under a blanket   a body unexplained
a coat and some other possessions nearby   a body
on the beach where the boat comes in and a cordon
around the waterfront   a body on the beach and
nobody looking for anyone else   a body on the beach
two women walking their dogs before sunrise
his life gone he comes ashore   a body entreating

By telegraph today, 9 a.m. New Plymouth S.E., fresh breeze, clouds passing, sea smooth. Manukau Heads S., fresh breeze, cloudy, bar clear of break. Auckland S.E., breeze, cloudy. Napier S.E., fresh breeze, overcast, sea smooth. Wellington S., light breeze, overcast, drizzling. Cape Farewell S.E., fresh breeze, misty, sea moderate. Lyttelton Calm, overcast. Port Chalmers N.E., breeze, gloomy. Bluff E., light breeze, clouds passing.

daybreak and the harness jingle interrupts
my vigil   an early boat for an early train   one side
of the isthmus to the other and this freight
we bring to the wharf at Onehunga   put me
in an applebox he said once but I made sure
it was heart rimu   a delivery order for southern ports
time rolls up as we run to the Heads   there was nothing
in farming in those days and he lost all his money
nine months in the shipping office then nothing
until the first teaching job at Tataraimaka   this is how
I will tell the story   a progress through schoolhouses
the family growing   the master who told his children
that Stratford upon Patea would become very famous
if they all learned a sonnet and a page of the dictionary
every day   *for the good of your immortal souls* he said
Regan Street Miranda Street Broadway   these have feet
in other places   can you bring them home   can you make
them your own   I will not tell of the black despair that sank him
the cankers and rages that took him from us   dead
at thirty-nine the salary gone and what am I to do

the road swings behind Kawhia
and into the King Country   Bosco
in Te Kuiti   Fat Pigeon in Piopio
the hill country with its rocky outcrops
the gorge with its slips and laid off corners
Awakino the black river and then the coast
on a good day the White Cliffs and sometimes
if the light is right   the distant blue cone
rising out of the northern bight
Mokau Mohakatino Tongaporutu   river
mouths flooded with whitebait in season
Ahititi luring the birds with signal fires
Mount Messenger carved away to nothing
Uriti no longer a flood valley   the prow
of the canoe   Urenui Onaero Waitara
Bell Block all smoothed away   the gateway
in front of us now   Waiwhakaiho
snow-fed and running towards the sea

By telegraph today, 9 a.m. New Plymouth S.E., light breeze, blue sky, sea smooth. Manukau Heads S., breeze, cloudy, bar clear of break. Auckland W.S.W., breeze. Napier Calm, clouds passing, sea smooth. Wellington N.W., light breeze, clouds passing. Cape Farewell N.W., light breeze, moderate gale, sea smooth. Lyttelton Calm, blue sky. Port Chalmers S.W., gale, cloudy. Bluff W.S.W., fresh breeze, cloudy.

all day I watch the coast   all night
the wheel of stars and the moon going down
in the west   the dream caught me again
though I pushed it away   the little boy with a black cat
in his arms   the river pool five feet deep   my screams
the warm bath that would not bring him back
I turned my back and he was gone   I let them play
by the river   I was busy with the baby   the house
two and a half chains from the river   he was trying
to throw the cat in   slipped and fell and we took him
to the cemetery above the river   Te Henui
where they are reopening the plot this morning
as the Gairloch waits for a pilot to bring her to port
and Maggie shepherds everyone from the house
into Mr Irvine's conveyance   that much we can afford
I put away my distress   I put away from me
the fire-burned eye the falling down the cries for help
I could not give on that side of the dark river
I will put him under the ground with our two small sons
and take the living children home by the afternoon train
their tears will dry   their roads lie open before them

in the Hua and Waiwhakaiho Block we look
for numbers that will lead to roads   or reserves
up under the mountain   walk around the old house
noticing for the first time intricately carved panelling
and an upright piano stepped and ridged
with ambuscades and enfilading fire   camphor chest
and wooden tea tray   retinal afterflash against
high ceilings   you can't see it from there   the voice
is firm   come over here   and from the other side
there they are   sky people arikirangi   leaning out
of their cumulus gaily painted and billowing   faces
from Trefeglwys faces from Hua   faces in a dream

By telegraph today, 9 a.m. New Plymouth S.W., light breeze, clouds passing, sea smooth. Manukau Heads N.W., fresh breeze, squally, bar clear of break. Auckland S.S.W., breeze, cloudy. Napier Calm, clouds passing, sea smooth. Wellington S., light breeze, cloudy. Cape Farewell S.E., light breeze, blue sky, sea smooth. Lyttelton S., fresh breeze, overcast. Port Chalmers S.W., moderate gale, passing showers. Bluff W.N.W., fresh breeze, clouds passing.

matapouri

the magpies come to the corner of the house
and talk all morning to the figure on the flag that hangs
on the orange wall   my fingers trace the sewn words
COME WIRELESS   a voice fills in the rest and flashes
from my good right eye   ALALU   give back the black and white
but it's the orange I want   morning sunlight on the wall
the birds and their qwardle   the bells in the painting
of KARANGAHAPE ROAD in a shed on the side of the hill

nothing more joyous than a dog in water   except two dogs
paddling along beside us in the waist-deep water   so clear
the estuary at full tide   feet sinking through sandy crusts
WHOA   the dogs turn back and we drift with the current   WHOA
to where waves are coming over the bar   WH-OA   soft landing
against the side of a sand bank   as in the dream one moment
out of my depth one moment a toe on the bottom   I open my eyes
underwater   so clear   everything as it should be   kicking along

post MERIDIAN the wall of sound is cicadas   the shade sail
flaps one manta wing on the hot concrete and I'm off   barefoot
to find the London planes whose whitewashed trunks
will lead me   step by step   out to the point   an ALLÉE
a path to walk ALONE   counting and listening   marking off
each tree there and back   the dog running free with her nose in
RABBITS   sharp gravel springy kikuyu   ALONE and seeing
the same pathway in moonlight under the morepork's loony call

Note

A family is a series of intersecting arcs, some boat-shaped, others vaults or canopies, still others vapour trails behind a mountain or light refracted through water. None is enclosed, all are in motion, springing away from one another or folding themselves around some spectral inverse of the shape they make against sea or sky.

When we were growing up on the north Taranaki coast there were sausages blackening on corrugated iron over a fire built on river stones, and then a Thermette heating water for tea or the murk our parents called instant coffee. It was simple enough: you wrapped the sausage in bread and cooled your burnt mouth with slugs of cordial, orange or green, from the half gallon that came out of the booze bag. By the time the parents were arranging cups and milk and nattering to each other, we were back in the river for a last swim or drifting along the water's edge breaking up finely sculpted terraces of black sand by jumping on them *one two three* and down they came in thick collapsing slices.

The rivers ran down to beaches covered in sea wrack. The further west we were, the richer the haul of pearly ram's horns, silvery paua or the striated shells we called sea eggs. Best of all was the trek at low tide across acres of boulders to where the rusted iron ribs of a wreck heaved up against the sky. This is the wreck I see when I read Mary Stanley's searing lamentation:

> Offshore, sea beached these wrecks, their ribs
> picked clean by seasons of salt, and here
> the raping wave is master at last.

No bell is burial. Shag and gull
preach their heresies over the drowned
and foundered derelicts no one mourns.

I didn't know then that the ribs and boiler on the rocks beyond Weld Road belonged to the SS *Gairloch*, wrecked on Timaru Reef one night in 1903, fortunately without loss of life. I didn't know that my great-grandparents travelled on the *Gairloch* and other coastal steamers connecting Taranaki with Auckland in the days before the roads went through. I certainly didn't know that Elizabeth Evans brought her husband's body from Auckland to New Plymouth aboard the *Gairloch* and that she buried him in Te Henui Cemetery the same day, 29 September 1891. But it seems fitting to wrap a volume of poems about these and other family configurations in a cover that speaks to some of the minutes, lost and found, of those intersecting arcs.